The Subterfuge

ALSO BY NGOZI OLIVIA OSUOHA

The Transformation Train
Letter to My Unborn
Sensation
Tropical Escape (with Amos O. Ojwang')
Fruits from the Poetry Planet
Poetic Grenade
Whispers of the Biafran Skeleton
Chains
Raindrops
Freeborn
Eclipse of Tides

The Subterfuge

a poetic meditation by
Ngozi Olivia Osuoha

Poetic Justice Books
Port St. Lucie, Florida

©2019 Ngozi Olivia Osuoha

book design and layout: SpiNDec, Port Saint Lucie, FL
cover design: Kris Haggblom

All rights reserved.

No part of this book may be used or reproduced in any manner whatsoever without written permission except in the case of brief quotations embodied in critical articles and reviews. Members of educational institutions and organizations wishing to photocopy any of the work for classroom use, or authors, artists and publishers who would like to obtain permission for any material in the work, should contact the publisher.

Printed in the United States of America.
Published by Poetic Justice Books
Port Saint Lucie, Florida
www.poeticjusticebooks.com

ISBN: 978-1-950433-30-8

FIRST EDITION
10 9 8 7 6 5 4 3 2 1

dedication

In memory of all the soldiers who lost their lives fighting insurgency especially in the northern part of Nigeria.

To all those soldiers who are truly committed to this course, the patriots and those who have paid the ultimate price. We appreciate.

To all the soldiers who have had their fair share of bullet wounds from this fight, including Chidozie Kingsley Nwaogu, from my hometown.

And most especially, to my Facebook friend and soldier, ISOR BARIDAKARA DEEZUA, who actually made me believe that this war is real. May God always be with you.

The Subterfuge

LOYALTY

It begins with loyalty
Even at the point of death
You obey every order
Even if it is murder.

Agility and flexibility
Always alert and ready
In service and when not
You protect your fatherland.

Your blood may spill
Even against your will,
Killing, fighting, defending
Hunger, thirst, want and need
Amidst boredom and loneliness
Surrounded by corpses of colleagues and enemies.

SPIRITED

Under the sun
In the rain
Caves, mountains, muds
Rivers, ponds, streams
They go, they fight, they march.

Discouragements and doubts
Fears, tears and nightmares
Scary dreams, imaginations
Yet they put up strength.

Sickness, they battle
They wobble in the spirit
But none may know
Because they must not.

Echoes of horrors
Scenes of calamities
Pages of atrocities
Stages of deaths,
They see, they fight, they struggle
They harden and harden
Until they no longer leather.

ORDERS

Age does not count
Service seriously does
Discipline, they call it.

Orders come from ladders
None to be questioned
Obey, obey and obedience
Obedience is the key.

Even body language is sin
Facial expression is unwanted,
Strict, stringent and ardent orders
You just have to obey.

Your culture, religion or belief
Your profession, craft or skill
Your talent, manners or dream
Whatever, does not count.

Orders reign and rain
Submission, allegiance all matter
Bloody or friendly orders
Forward or backward
You dare not thwart.

Ngozi Olivia Osuoha
RELIGIOUS BRETHREN

Those in same religion embrace
They gather and meet,
They pray and preach
They propagate their religion.

The others in other religions do
They fight for supremacy
They flaunt superiority
They live large and proud.

Religion; numerous and influential
Major ones loudly roar
Minor ones poorly crawl,
Silent ones sleep
Unknown ones die
For all, they care.

Religion amidst camouflage
Bloody, cunning, deceitful
Crazy, taking certain things for granted
Lazy, believing things would be favourable.

Love goes right beyond
Hate spreads left beneath,
Disunity spilling
Resentment nurturing.

ALLEGIANCE

Younger ones pledge allegiance
Allegiance to Senior ones
As seniors rule like God.

This seniority is dictatorship
The spirit of gun, ordering
The zeal of leadership, hunting.

Guns, fighting
Orders, scaring
Contemplation, gingering.

No challenge, no argument
No report, no support
No demonstration, no protest
Like sacrificial lambs, they move
They walk ever to their slaughter.

Ngozi Olivia Osuoha

TRIBALISM

Tongues and tribes divide
Clans and kinsmen unite,
Motives and interests shield
Tribalism, hunting friendliness.
Brothers cooking together
Relatives, wining and dining
Strangers; scapegoats.

Promotions cheer kingdoms
Kingdoms cheer promotions,
Friends pursuing goals
Cliques advancing
Nobodies, rising, falling and rising.

Tribalism, sabotaging
Hate, laying snares
Power abusing rights
Ranks trapping, capturing.

Tongues and tribes dividing
Tribes and tongues, severing
Bitterness, quest, rivalry dominating.

MARGINALIZATION

Minorities fade away
Insignificance, fed up
Majorities blossom,
Significance boom.

Juniors get trapped
Young ones get stock
Stranded ones hit grid
Confused sets get lost.

Marginalization, segregation
Discrimination, retaliation
Boundaries, shores, lines
From up to down
From down to top,
Backward, forward
Left, right, center.

Segregation beyond words
Marginalization beyond acts
Jealousy, envy, camouflage
Punishment in the face of discipline.

Ngozi Olivia Osuoha

SALARY

Peanuts for peasants
Poor incentives
Dead allowances
Decayed bonuses
Stunted growth.

Late payment
Half motivation
Diminished morale
Buried zeal.

Gloomy passion
Dark courage
Red hope
Wild danger,
Wide death.

Unguaranteed safety
Poor defence
Punctured tires
Frightening orders
Suspicious errand
Committed pathway
Bought death trap.

No salary, not with it
Peasant, peanut
Unpleasant, unconducive.

Unfair package
Unkind pocket
Unfriendly purse,
Unfamiliar packs.

Salary, waiting, cracking
Tormenting, teargassing
Salary, a tip of an ice Berg.

ILLITERACY

Greater percentage of illiteracy
Tearing down some respect
As though it is for dropouts.

Those who may not value lives
Those who look down on credentials
Those who know not the pain;
The worth, the sacrifice of academics.

As credentials may earn envy
It may bring jealousy, anger
Because they neither understand nor appreciate.

Clearly, there is a difference
Crystal, it shines
But then, who truly recounts
The rages of the heart.

Ngozi Olivia Osuoha

HARSH TRAINING

Harsh training upon training
Morning, afternoon, night
Sunny, rainy days.

Some die, some wound
Some harden, some vow
Trainings, inhumane and harsh.

Building them for themselves
Building them against others
Destroying love, sanity and sanctity.

Trainings that pull strengths
Trainings that push minds
Trainings that fight spirits
Harsh trainings that kill flesh.

Deaths, wound, sickness, breakdowns
Cramps, muscle pull, tears and sprain
These and many more struggles
Battling the camouflage against itself.

PUNISHMENT

Minor things to be ignored
Silly jokes to be laughed over
Pranks to be overlooked
Tricks to be forgotten,
These cause problems.

Straight face, serious action
Senior jokes, mature plays
Real talks, strict orders
Official works, nothing but struggle.

Like a jungle, like a dungeon
Slightest anomaly equals guardroom,
Poorest slight, very questionable
Detention, punishment, hard labour.

Ngozi Olivia Osuoha

LEADERSHIP

Leaders pave the way
They direct and coordinate
They protect and guide
They guard and sacrifice.

Leaders lead, they lead by example
Leaders mann and defend
They are gods, they god the people.

Leaders, be they dwarfs or giants
Be they deaf or dumb, blind or lame
Leaders, no matter how be they
And where they be, are heroes.

Lives depend on them
Souls lean on them
Spirits thrive on their words
Minds create from their legacies,
Needless be they saboteurs.

Leaders define leadership
They must not trade on blood
Neither must they trample on lives.

But leaders, many of them
Turn out to be wolves rather than shepherds.

GOVERNMENT

Sometimes, governments do harm
They suffer and hurt the governed.

Sometimes, governments go blind
They neither see nor read the people.

Sometimes, governments become lame
They neither see nor rescue the people.

Sometimes, governments cause war
They kill the people they govern.

Sometimes, governments make rules
Rules that are against the populace.

Sometimes, governments ignore the polity
They heat it up, at all cost.

Sometimes, governments do businesses
Businesses unknown to their citizens,
Many a time, governments betray the land.

Ngozi Olivia Osuoha

GREED

Greed has become laws
Laws, ruling and ruining lives.

Leaders are too greedy
They pocket, milk and syphon.

Representatives are selfish
They encircle themselves,
Their families or nothing else.

Councillors are crooks
They deceive and deny
They withhold and steal.

Leadership is now a camouflage
It misguides, misrules, misleads
Governance is no longer honourable
It misconstrues, misinforms, miseducates
Greed, is the table of the banquet.

Selfish people all over rulership
Fighting tooth and nail,
Barricading and blocking
Killing, maiming, kidnapping
No one is safe, the land is quaking.

Greed, the true leader
The ruler of the rulers
And the king of the universe.

POVERTY

Poverty on the throne
Ruling the masses
Killing the land.

Lies and white lies
Cheap popularity on paper,
Signatures and contracts
All, a bunch of fakery.

Poverty on rampage
Wasting talents and dreams
Dividing destinies and passions.

Poor people are thieves
Rich people are honourables.

Stolen wealth, embezzled funds
Looted treasuries, squandered ministries.

BUSINESS

Smart ones do business
Clever ones cover up
Diverted funds, money laundering.

Cliques and cells
Chains and cabals
Groups and links
Businesses thrive on heads.

Informants miss, monitors disappear
Heads roll, blood spill
Businesses, boom.

Secret meetings, closed door dates
Oaths of secrecy, oaths of allegiance
Businesses compound, so complexly.

Beyond the ordinary, underneath the carpet
Hunger, misery, poverty, evil loom.

INFILTRATION

Strangers become families
Undercovers turn passionate
Spies multiply.

Obedience and allegiance
Discipline and loyalty
Calm and tranquil
Integrity and humanity
Many more, in a bid to fire.

Across climes and lands
Smuggled by the caucus
Supported by the chamber
Protected by the inner house
All works must be done.

Central link serving the server
The server servicing generality,
Numbers, so ignorant
Numbers so loyal, so dedicated.

Ngozi Olivia Osuoha
MERCENARY

Mercenaries hidden and open
Fighting for private gains
Political, religious, social
Economic, financial, academic.

Mercenaries fighting for their masters
Putting their lives on the line,
Some happily, some grudgingly.

Blowing up people and places
Messing up lives and lands.

Mercenary, a tool of interest
Known how best to be used by users.

Mercenary, fates interwoven
Mines interlocked in a grid,
A grid of diverse colours.

INFORMANTS

Informants, risky breed
Sourcing, searching, spreading information.

This set lays snares
As many as possible.

This group plays smart
As much as possible.

They are at risk, doing a risky job
They get trapped sometimes.

Informants, many depend on them
Sometimes, they depend on others
Sometimes, they play, they fall.

Hide and seek, seek and hide
They mount pressures and tensions,
They ease them too, sometimes.

False news is treacherous
False alarm is sabotage,
Care, careful, carefulness,
Yet, what will be will be.

FOREST

Sleeping in the forest
Waking in the bushes
Living in trenches
Dying in mountains,
These soldiers, sacrifice a lot.

Lonely, with guns
Facing lions, beasts and burdens
Fighting many devils
Waiting to die or live.

Like lambs on sacrificial lane
Loyal, quiet, dumb
Serving a purpose; so strange.

These forests become their home
Shelter, roof, bed, warmth, love
Living, dying, mourning, living.

Wandering and wondering
Wailing and weeping
Yet, fighting to live.

Protecting unknown people
Safekeeping a strange land
Defending the unborn.

SELFISHNESS

Greed breeds selfishness
Selfishness begets jealousy
Jealousy brews envy
Envy, hibernates covetousness.

Anger and rape, bitterness and hate
All for me, no other person
Monies, arms, alms, tours.

Self-defense, self satisfaction
Self promotion, self presentation
Self management, self appeasing
Self, self, self, selfishness,
Nothing but self.

The camouflage is a green snake
A green snake on a green grass
Biting, spitting, poisoning, killing
As many as possible, far and near.

Ngozi Olivia Osuoha

RANK

Ranks ranking raw
Ranking according to wishes
Promoting friends and families
Hoarding rivals and opposition.

The camouflage is like a leopard
Spotted in colours
Like the Tigger, lion and zebra
Different lines and designs
Doing many killings.

Rank, a prank in a tank
As safe as a bank,
But have many, sank.

Ranking, ranks and files
Tearing files across niles
Banking and thanking miles
The rank, a set of camouflage.

SACRIFICE

Life notwithstanding
As living on the line,
The ultimate price glittering
As some sacrifice others.

The sacrifice beyond freewill
Facing, luring, compelling
Compounding, aggravating, pushing
A sacrifice that is always worthy.

Dead, forgotten, gone, unmourned
Served or not, unremembered
Sweat and service, buried
Sacrifice, a camouflage in red.

Lamb for the slaughter
Blood for the land
Great, wasted sacrifice.

Ngozi Olivia Osuoha

WOUNDED

Many wounded in the front line
There ends their career
For they die or rot with it.

Useless, as they may be
None remembers, nor helps
As they beg for alms.

Half treatment sometimes
Part payment sometimes
Then abandoned
The camouflage, a subterfuge of reality.

Wounded men, wounded women
Brave troops, gallant soldiers
Battling, bedridden, in camouflage.

RETIRED

Retired servicemen in pain
Starving to live one next day
Unpaid gratuities and pensions
Camouflage, the spotted leopard.

Left the barracks in peace or shame
But hunger is sure,
Leaving with memories
Living in realities
Camouflage, a spotted lion.

Some wasted strengths
Some wasted lives,
Some bound dreams
Some killed visions
All in long flash
Camouflage, a spotted zebra.

Ngozi Olivia Osuoha
POLITICS

Politics, my wayward brother
A tetra headed dragon
A coat of many colours,
It came and things changed.

Politics, politics of doom
Pranking on lives, tricking souls
Tormenting groups, torturing visions
Strangling and antagonizing dreamers.

Politics, from top to bottom
Dribbling arms, penetrating channels
Meandering, gallivanting, salivating
Horrible politics, of life and death.

Greed, money, fame, security
Master, mastery, dupe, dubious
Free, greediness, vengeance, vengefulness
Vindictive, barbaric, demonic, satanic.

GAME

Like draft, chess and Scrabble
They play with humans
Like football, basketball and handball
They toss with skulls.

Game, deep, going deeper
A web of crazy nuts
Tightening by the day
Conscripting, constipating, conspiring.

Like lawn tennis, they go to court
Playing with families,
They kick, play and score
Scoring scores of baskets
Fountains, yes, fountains of blood overflowing.

Leisurely, conveniently and comfortably
They play at the expense of others.

Ngozi Olivia Osuoha

FALL OUT

Fallouts of diverse angles
Connecting links of various types
Struggles of coverups
Quest for winning,
Complex; inferior and superior
Supremacy, power tussles
Within and without,
Souls, washing away.

Intra, infra, supra, Indra
Interior, exterior, ulterior, posterior
Clearances, clarity, charities, anomalies
Closures, foreclosures, measures, pressures,
Seizures, pleasures, postures, sutures,
Mini, maxi, poor, rich, hidden, glaring,
And the compounded certificates.

Fallouts; poisonous, corrosive, contagious
Staining hands, soiling lands, desecrating altars
The camouflage, a thorn in the flesh.

EMBEZZLEMENT

The top bulldozes
The head tears down,
The neck, supports
The hands, buttress
The legs, speed up
The eyes go blind
The lips keep mute
The ears go deaf
The buttucks sit on them all.

Millions under carpet
Billions syphoned
Trillions exported
Uncountable lost.

Manpower, resources, priorities, pledges
Aim, interest, motive, motto, belief
Efforts and all others,sabotaged.

Ngozi Olivia Osuoha

CONSPIRACY

Forces unite, exploding
Collisions, blowing up
No friction, no gravity
And accompanying several nods.

Conspiracy, upon conspiracies
Cabals upon cabals
Cabals for cabals, cabals against cabals
With them, together and in unison
Conspirators conspiring constant calamities.

The unborn weeping and wailing
The living dying and mourning
The dead wandering and wondering
Conspiracy, conspiracy of silence.

INTRUDERS

Secretly, they come
Trespassing to the unknown
Winding beyond silence
Wrecking havoc.

Quietly, they advance
Taking over gradually,
Occupying against normality.

From a drop to drops
Companies, companions
Accomplices and partners
Moving up to the floodgates.

They advance, they run over
They gradually announce a take over
Like a coup, like a fight
The struggle becomes real.

THREATS

Jokingly, their presence threatens
Expanding beyond strangers
Invading communities, towns
Scaring, pressuring, pressurizing, intimidating
Then comes the ugly message.

Threats, upon threats
Traditionally, culturally, religiously
Locally, naturally, internationally
Losses, killings, maimings, murders
Butchering, destructions, and deaths.

They threaten so loud, so real
Gaining voice and momentum
Chasing indigenes, erasing tracks
The threats pour in numbers.

FEARS

It looms, looming and lurking
Fears grip, grabbing the land
Confusion and commotion
Doubts and wondering
Of what is to come.

The past, the present, the future
The deeds, the doings, the will-dos
Fears parade day and night.

Aliens and talibans
Masquerades and ghosts
Spirits and demons
Tormenting humans in broad daylights.

Forward ever, backward never
Backward ever, forward never
All wonder the fate of the night.

Ngozi Olivia Osuoha

CHALLENGE

Indigenous and strangers
Fighting and killing
Strangers trampling and tearing down
With force in full force
Crushing and cutting down.

Strangers challenging aborigines
Throwing a challenge party,
Killing with impunity
Tending to have immunity,
Blood flowing ceaselessly.

Morning, afternoon, night
Terrors whistling and roaring
Mounting up in heaps
Charging the gaps of cruelty.

LINKS

Linking up with breeds
Gathering birds of same feathers
Fraternities, in nooks and crannies,
Outrageous rampage with guts.

Indoctrinating, inculcating, inhabiting
Nurturing, initiating, fantasizing
Dogmas; pulling down strongholds
Destroying riverbanks and bonds,
Permeating and perforating
Puncturing, suturing and injuring
Cracking up and pushing down
Burning homes and families
Mesmerizing kindred spirit.

Links to foreign terrors
Connections to local horrors
Bounds and boundaries collapsing.

FRATERNITY

Brotherhoods in diverse forms
Secret, open, physical, mental
Moral, financial, societal, religious
Camouflaging, sabotaging, playing hide and seek.

Fraternities of young and old
Beings of great and small
Fighting for, against, with and in
Pretending to be in tune.

Cockerels and bulldogs
Spiders and scorpions
Cancers and cankerworms
Cohorts and coordinators
Piercing, tracing, weaving and fomenting trouble.

TERRORISM

Ugly beliefs against mankind
Cruel breeding and training
Whitewashing and brainwashing
Fierce danger and gang ups
Raging like hurricanes
Scrapping lands, troubling waters.

Bombing, killing, capturing, beheading
Raping, defiling, devouring,
Beasts sacrificing humans
Scavengers, picking and picking lives.

Terrorism becoming norms
Terrorists turning crusaders
Terrors and wars, harm and evil
Countless groups countering peace
Numerous units shattering unity
Unknown voices silencing prayers.

Ngozi Olivia Osuoha

ORGANIZED CRIME

Men of physical strength
In their primes and greens
Willing to kill and be killed
In uniform, ammunitions and trainings.

Promises made, monies paid
Pledges took, oaths administered
Allegiance, bonds and unions
All and many appearing stronger.

The more you look, the less you see
Jokes, plays, dramas, dilemmas, and traumas
Stage, performances, stage managed
All looking like organized crime,
The camouflage, camouflaging.

BUSINESS VENTURES

They say it is business
They say it is a venture
They say it is an enterprise
They say it is a competition
They say it is war
They say it is power tussle
They call it end time.

Some blame amalgamation
Some blame diversity
Some point at illiteracy
Some say it is ignorance,
But many rumour business.

Business with lives, lands and hopes
Sacrifices of the highest order
They shoot, they choose, they merry
They segregate, they pride, they manage.

The camouflage, the sabotage
The subterfuge, all nothing but business.

Ngozi Olivia Osuoha

AGREEMENT

Shoot this day, kill this number
Rest today, and bomb tomorrow
Fire from dawn till dawn
Raze hundreds of homes.

One by one, bit by bit
Two by two, three by three
Today, and tomorrow
Rest on the following day.

Wait, let the news be heard
Let the world mourn as we party
Pay me twice, I will deliver real.

Before the mourning is over
Hit again and again and again
Let the doom be very gloomy,
Remember agreement is agreement.

SABOTAGE

The camouflage flaunts
Boasting of power
Displaying might and zeal
But underneath is a cancer
A cankerworm eating it deep,
Milking almost a skeleton
Enjoying on the flesh.

Ants, tiny ants
Invading elephants
Biting, eating, drinking, spilling
Pulling down giants.

Saboteurs envying sabotage
Camouflage in the midst of camouflage
Pretence, deceit, betrayal
A dive, diving derivatives,
A driver, driving paradigm
A drone dropping sophisticated arsenal.

Ngozi Olivia Osuoha
ETHNIC CLEANSING

Glittering traces of killing
Pointing accusations and allegations
Pictures of ethnic cleansing.

Definite tribes and voices
Assassinations and silences
Silencing threats and likely threats.

Answers being erased
Witnesses thrown into seas
Evidences swept away
Everything doubtful, illusive and deceptive.

Ethnic cleansing, loud and clear
Crystal to the blind
Fears of the unknown,
As heads roll, roofs raze
Certain tribes vanish into oblivion.

FRUSTRATIONS

Better hands get chopped off
Stronger heads crack
Weaker souls divide
Feeble kneels bend
Poor groups starve
Innocent men die.

Frustrations up and down
Failures, left and right
Seizures, front and back
Tensions, roundabouts.

Traps and traps
Nets and nets
Webs and webs
Tricks, pranks, disguises
Confusion, complexity, clashes
Ladders, carders, ranks all engrossed.

Ngozi Olivia Osuoha

ARCHAIC WEAPONS

Ancient weapons, old and outdated
Archaic and museum-like arsenal
Dilapidated ammunitions
Good for nothing, almost
Running to meet terror.

Backward mindset, fear of defeat
Shortage, outage, loss, hunger, sickness
Sacrifices of death signature
Intentional suffering and hardship
The camouflage, an unwritten page.

Inferior equipment, Manning the gate
Superior warfare scrapping the fate
Interior danger looming within
Exterior dagger beheading like sin.

ENEMY'S HAND

Illiterate enemy willing to die
Ready to be sainted in heaven
To be decorated by angels
And be adorned with virgins,
Garnishing blood upon the land.

The enemy's hand, red and black
Fierce crimson, dark and ungodly
Outpouring of evil
Crude venting of unnecessary anger
Raw passion and determination
Outrageous will to kill and or be killed.

Ragged, rag-tag, dirty, rude and nude
Unlearned, unsafe, unapologetic
Brainwashed by greedy apes
Betting on them, strategizing
Drafting and paddling demonic canoes.

Ngozi Olivia Osuoha

UNPATROTIC

When monies are released
Ranks file them
Piling them up in foreign lands
Cruising in jets and helicopters,
Buying toys to fight terrorism
The camouflage, a vultures of dirtiness.

Unpatriotic gallows, dug for truth
Greedy graves harbouring loyalists
Selfish prisons locking heroes
Lustful jails rusting legends.

The camouflage, an anthem of hypocrisy
Cutting and bending corners
Doing unthinkable things.

WHITE LIES

White lies in broad daylights
Shinning like armours
Glittering and dazzling
Like silver and diamond.

White lies told by ranks
Covering up open secrets
Hiding the moon, sealing the sun
Wedging rain, darkening snow.

They lie openly, without shame
Shamelessly, they conspire
They gather at round tables
Even when tables are upside down.

The camouflage, an empty pot
Cooking nothing, rather burning all.

Ngozi Olivia Osuoha

PAPER VICTORY

Victory on paper
Defeat in news
Conquest on air,
Vanquished on grounds.

Paper victory, a white lie
The blue chip that leaks
The blueprint from the beginning.

One obvious lie that cannot be hidden
Amounts to thousands of harm sealed
Victory song, conquest band
Defeat alarm, vanquished memorial.

The camouflage, a band of rootless men
Seeking to agonize, antagonize
Desperate to destroy.

DRAFT

Drafted kidnap
Mapped rescue mission
Innocent messengers
A play to raise fund.

Heads, skulls and skeletons
Heaps of corpses, stinking race
Pack of cards, Kings and queens
The hustle is real
The tussle is dark,
The jungle is barbaric.

A camouflage, chameleon
Colourful, a bitter lemonade
Acidifying honey
Toxicifying breath
Drafts, a joke and play
To those who enjoy it.

Ngozi Olivia Osuoha

NEIGHBOURING COUNTRIES

Taken by neighbours
Neighbours of coasts and shores
Borders that are poisonous
Porous boundaries that swallow.

Neighbouring countries, becoming demonic
Possessed by murdering spirits
Killing people in their ancestral homes
Terrorising giants; brothers and sisters.

A hand to scatter, shatter and batter
Jealousy and envy, paid and sent
Used, abused, misused and misled
Bought to inflict pain, perpetual pain.

The camouflage, a coat of many colours
Looking like rainbow
But a radioactive fallout.

LOCAL

Some locals in ascending voice
Consenting to terror
Destroying their homes and lands
Fighting against their opponent,
Believing in missionary.

Local powers tormenting locals
Invading peace and unity
Demolishing pillars, pillars of love.

Local mentality, blinding crude and minds
Tying them to perpetual slavery
Flogging them to death.

Locals, deviating from norms
Watering hate and tribalism
Injecting disunity in the unborn
The camouflage, a disdain.

NATIONAL

Nationals, scattering the nation
Fighting for national cake
Dragging the owner, the user and keeper.

Nationals, disobeying constitutions
Abusing laws and orders
Segregating, discriminating, marginalizing
National voices speaking against the people.

Masses in bondages, serving in solitude
Sleeping and waking up in death,
Eating and drinking starvation
Merrying in hunger, and thirst
The camouflage, a national disgrace.

National heroes in shame
National leaders shameless
Old and aged ancestors chanting war.

INTERNATIONAL

And there they are
Blowing and heating up
Trying to part the land
Using insiders and outsiders.

Predicting, prophesying, envisaging
Giving dates, signs and wonders
Working and hoping towards them all.

Wolves in sheep's clothing
Portraying help, but devourers
Confusing the land
Confiscating resources
Twisting unions, truncating fates.

Planting discord, curbing peace
Beating war drums, giving dangerous alarms
Blowing hot air, warming troubles
Fermenting and fomenting enmity
International camouflage, a green snake.

Ngozi Olivia Osuoha

BOSS

Of the bosses that order
Officially in office, relaxing
Fielding poor and young
Drafting green and tender
Enjoying posts and not duty posts.

Positions of fame and honour
Indicting accusing fingers
Implicating subordinates
Maltreating immediate replacements
Misapplying, misappropriating, misgiving.

The boss of less trust
Digger of pain and rain
Golddigger and joy killer
Unfriendly friend, in camouflage.

Lo, he comes and goes
Salutes, salutations and respect
Honour, dignity, pride and orderliness
Lo, the shameless boss.

ANGER

Miserable anger through the ladder
Jealousy of no equation
Rivalry and competition
Yet order, discipline and timing.

Pull him down syndrome
Except in the clique
Tear him to pieces
Except in the cabal
The camouflage, deceiving greenness.

You dare not grow
Neither do you outgrow
You dare not spread
Neither do you outspread
Just be a dummy
A toy in the hands of children
Be a ball in the field of players
The camouflage, the highest stage of manipulation.

Hidden anger, open anger
Nervous hate, secret wish to overthrow,
A subterfuge of embedded colours.

Ngozi Olivia Osuoha

WASTE

Wasting intelligence
Crushing brilliance
Killing smartness
Auctioning cleverness
Waylaying neatness
Ambushing godliness.

The camouflage, a waste of reality
Beaming up the struggle
Supporting the jungle
Increasing loss and defeat
Stitching backwardness.

Waste of time and energy
Abuse of resources and materials
A set up against the land
Burning up, tearing down
Killing, attacking, terrorizing
A set against peace
Against evens and odds
The breakthrough that breaks hearts
The break-even that burns souls,
A love that hates life
The subterfuge, a clone of peaceful war.

UNCEASING WAR

Wars of no just cause
Wars of no just course,
Wars of no just curse
Rains of bullet, roundabout.

Incessant business, money making machine
Cartels and lagoons, producing ammunitions
Countries and heads selling weapons
Suckling, sucking people dry
Licking blood and sands
Trumpeting peace, yet;
Moguls of arsenals.

Even when peace arrives
Or anything that looks like peace,
They disrupt her
They rape and mourn her
They sink and send her back
They behead her
They force her to bear a stillbirth
They make sure she dies prematurely
And they stage a protest in her honour.

A camouflage that darkens
A subterfuge that shines like gold
Pure sabotage, raw and undiluted.

Ngozi Olivia Osuoha

ALLIES

Allies in many forms
Giving secret supports
Supporting both the enemy and the friend
Teaming up with all to destroy all.

Lies, traps, tactics and methods
Strategies, patterns, systems
Unthinkable techniques,
Unimaginable processes
Unbelievable procedures
Cooking doom and loom
Happily executing, manifesting.

Allies, aligning for and against
Alluring the lost and found
Allotting problems proportionally
Allocating fumes of death
Apportioning troubles proportionately
Amalgamating issues directly
Aligning deceits indirectly
Swinging pendulums of camouflage
Dancing balls of stoppers
The pointer, the stopwatch, the resonance
All, wondrous subterfuge.

BRIBERY

Bribing their way through
Shutting up obstacles
Clearing hindrances
Money, lands, properties
Vacations, offers, promises.

Bribery, a roping net
Receive and die
Reject and die
Talk and disappear
Expose and melt
Hide and vanish
Keep mute and be muted,
Camouflage and subterfuge,
Subterfuge, that camouflages.

The camouflage, a stage, a dance
A performance that bewilders
A wonderment of plenty maze
A cycle of distrust, fear and danger.

Bribes, bribery, set ups, and dirty deals
The connecting link that entangles lives
Lives of a people, nation, and land,
In short that of the world at large,
Camouflage, a green snake on a green grass.

Ngozi Olivia Osuoha

CORRUPTION

Enticing innocent ones
And setting them up too,
Advocating juicy offers
Yet blackmailing them.

Corrupt saints
Interrupting their missions
Corrupting angels
Disrupting their messages
Extorting, distorting
Twisting, intertwining, interweaving
Curling and entangling destinies.

Corrupt minds administrating
Dirty hands, healing
Contaminated heads, heading
Censored ears, hearing
Dented priests, atoning.

The camouflage, the siege of corruption
Bribery, corruption, sabotage and subterfuge
Counter chorus orchestrating
Noisy melody, humming
Loud cries, singing
A deceptive tank; receptive.

ASSASSINATION

The way things happen
In recessional succession
Or successive recession
The way deaths occur like planned
Calculated, meditated, premeditated and unanimous
One cannot but tag it assassination.

Timbers and calibres
Giants and Irokos
Cell leads and chain heads
Dropping dead one by one
According to number, accusations, allegations.

At some point, some knew their ends
At some other points, they pretend
Assassination of character
Defamation, indictment
Assassination of life, threats, and threats
Family kidnapping, ransom and ransom;
A wet feather that hardly flies.

Subterfuge, camouflage, sabotage
Sabotaging saboteurs
Camouflaging camouflager.

Ngozi Olivia Osuoha

TERRORISTS

Dedicated terrorists
Dying in favour
Dying in honour
Willing for the sacrifice
Ready for the freedom,
Bombing and blowing up everywhere
Schools, churches, mosques, markets, parks
Killing scores, and as many as possible.

Suicide bombers in numbers
Gunmen in numbers
Well armed, seem well sponsored
Eager, curious, enthusiastic
Interested, passionate, zealous
Appearing locally, nationally, internationally.

Breeds of unfathomable beliefs
Kinds of innumerable convictions
Loyal, steadfast, trustworthy, focused,
Tearing and burning the camouflage.

SPONSORS

Realities on ground prove real
Evidences at sight say so
Sponsors abound,
Supporters are limitless
Pillars and founders
Patrons and patron saints
Pushing, advising, advancing, administering.

Ghost, invisible sponsor
Spiritual fathers, political godfathers
Religious backgrounds, social base
Razing the camouflage.

The camouflage in subterfuge
A sabotage of dark pleasure
Bouncing, renouncing and abounding.

Sponsors sponsoring censored
Censors censoring uncensored
Tutors doctoring monitors
The camouflage, sights and sounds of war.

Ngozi Olivia Osuoha

BATTLE

Heavy battles within and without
Fierce war, unconventional
Suspicious and conspicuous
The camouflage in battle with self.

Battles, war fronts and front lines
Crazy and irrational killings
Canterchorus defense on the dense
Despair, solitude, bondage and mess.

Fights fighting ugly nights
Nights finding untidy fights,
Beautiful souls in drains
Humane spirits in trenches
Deaths of holy bands
Bodies of mutual colleagues
Decaying like compost manure
Camouflaging patriotism and defense.

Battles of heavy axes
Axing camouflage and subterfuge
Saboteurs and subterfuge
Picking interest in loss.

CHAMELEON

Colours of all shades
Shades of all colours
Supporting the enemy
Fighting for the camp,
One leg in, one leg out
Coalition and collisions
The subterfuge, numerous colours.

Dissemination of information
Within the enemy camp
Ringing the alarm
Within their territory
The camouflage, a chameleon of wonders.

Targets and points of meetings
Centers of circumnavigation
Adventures of lust and materials
Selling the camp, buying the land
Auctioning for the foe
O camouflage, a treacherous chameleon.

Ngozi Olivia Osuoha

POLITICAL INTEREST

Drafting for power
Swearing to retain it
Debating to overturn
Political interest, the camouflage.

Deals and dates of ugly trend
Books and records of bushy views
Eagerness and meanness
Quest for destruction
Politics, my wayward brother.

Oaths to kill if not elected
Covenants to war if not compensated
Incitements and sponsorings
Sponsorships and scholarships
Vindictiveness, violence, violation
Humiliation and total aggrandizement.

The camouflage, a piece of rag
Shabby, raggy, dirty unclean
Stuffy, noisy, suffocating.

RAMPAGE

At a point, it triggers
It becomes a rampage
Stampede, taking over
Covering up the hand
Getting all worried and concerned
None is safe, none is strong
No matter the alertness
All, fears and prays.

Yet, people are somewhere, happy
Toasting to insecurity and death
Wining and dining to imbalance
Causing more harm
Unleashing more terror and doom
Advancing in destruction
Empowering war, advocating mayhem.

The camouflage is a face value
Coining a palatable meal
Warming up, but sleeping
As lions roar and devour.

Ngozi Olivia Osuoha

UNCONDITIONAL WAR

A war is on
A mighty war
Quaking the earth
Sliding the land
Ravaging lives and properties
But hardly to be won.

Unconventional war
A war of uncertainties
A war of faceless brides
A fight of ghosts and grooms
Separating lands and climes,
Yet uniting them.

Evil outgoing good
Devil celebrating victory
Demons, elaborating feasts
Monsters hosting banquets
Vultures filling, hauls filing
Bones and flesh, manure
The land outpouring blood.

MUTINY

Angry birds fly
Tormented doves stray
Tortured eagles soar
They face mutiny.

Decent sheep petition
Godly breed intervene
Lowly lamb intercede
They face mutiny.

In their numbers, they pray
In their best, they plea
In their desire, they proceed
In their prayers, they stand
They face mutiny.

Courtmarshalled, court marshalling
Being killed by the friend
Being butchered by the enemy
Left, right, front, back, center
Up, down, roundabout, unsafe.

Ngozi Olivia Osuoha

TREASON

Suggestions for growrh
plenaries for development
Petitions for movements
Submissions for liberty
Points for freedom
They face treason.

Rights, activism, liberties
Voices, associations, cultures
They face treason.

Caged, sacrificed, sabotaged
Deceived, hanged, wasted
Untraceable, unseen, unknown
Unmentioned, unaccounted, undisclosed
They faced treason.

Secret, invader, open concealer
Unheard killer, enemy within
For us, against us, before us
The camouflage, the land of horror.

ENEMY AID

When you aid the enemy
He kills you deeper
Throwing down food from planes
Buying and using lesser drones
Treating them preferentially, then.

They gain access to information
Stronger intelligence report
Informants, sponsorship, freedom
Dialogue, amnesty and promises.

Favour, favouritism, backup, support
Nepotism, tribalism, lurings, lobbies, offers
Better equipments, giving them voice.

Enemy aiding, enemy aiders
Strong protection, hard coverings
Trade by barter, dramatic
Amidst traumas on families.

Ngozi Olivia Osuoha

MASS GRAVES

Terrorism beyond control
Tearing them into rags
Shredding flesh and bones.

Mass graves of men and women
Killing beyond understanding
Graves, upon graves
Secret, and hidden
Open and loud.

Mass graves of soldiers
Mass graves of civilians
Men, women, children
Cutting across religions and beliefs.

Eyesores, heartbreaks, bizaires
Nightmares, taboos and abormination
Terrors, wars, fights, clashes
Deceit, play, unknown realities
Mass graves, an indelible ugly legacy.

DEATH SENTENCE

Bare hands do not kill ghosts
Bare feet do not march down spirits
Better equipments do better jobs
Sophisticated arms fight sophisticatedly,
Bare soldier can do less.

Death sentence for mutiny, treason
Rebellion, withdrawal, or lots more
Death sentence, death sentence we hear
Terrors and terrorists living at large.

Terrorists being reintegrated
Recruited, absorbed, rehabilitated,
All we hear
Soldiers; hungry, angry, ill-armed
Being killed, being sentenced, being played.

Crazy drafts and draftings
Ethnic cleansing, they rumour
Political dramas, we hear
The camouflage, the subterfuge
The subterfuge, the camouflage.

Ngozi Olivia Osuoha

LANDMINES

Landmines over there
Exploding at will,
Triggers around
Corking at will
Bombs, grenades and explosives
Killing as many as possible.

Loved ones, worried
Relatives, in fear
Homes, lonely and bored
Deaths hovering round and around.

Landmines, in camouflage
Camouflage, in landmines
Sabotaging landmines;
Landmarks as subterfuge.
Landmines planted
Seen, unseen, known, unknown
Enemy within, enemy without
For us and against us.

DANCE AND PYTHON

Down here, they dance
Pythons, strangling and conscripting
Felling young men, able bodied
Wasting blood and lives.

Yes, down here they dance
Willingly, forcefully, proud and bold
Tormenting and torturing
Able bodied men, disappearing.

Down here, pythons dance
Crawling, moving, noon and night
Swallowing lives and dreams.

Pythons are not domestic
But roar like lions
Devouring, demeaning and dehumanizing.

Ngozi Olivia Osuoha

SMILING CROCODILES

Yes, no tears at all
They smile around here
Smiling at criers
Laughing at mourners
Mourners and criers
Weepers and wailers
Those, whom they devoured.

Yes, the crocodiles smile loud
Loud at bodies and corpses
Dancing, partying
Swimming in waters
Waters, running South.

Smiling crocodiles
Dancing pythons,
All keep their corridors safe up there,
For a camouflaging force.

SAFETY OF THEIR CORRIDOR

Safeguarding their corridor
Protecting their parlour
Safekeeping their ward
Shepherding their cattle
Enriching their home
Building their barn
Yes, their corridor must be safe.

As long as the python dances
Dances in the east
As far as the crocodile smiles
Smiles in the south
The corridor must be safe in the north.

But the sun rises in the east
And sets in the west,
As waters run down south
It leaves the north, dry.

Hear, see, feel, taste
Hear the sabotage
Feel the camouflage
See the subterfuge
Complex web of tactical mixture.

Ngozi Olivia Osuoha

DIALOGUE

They dialogue proudly
Shamelessly, while killing the unarmed
They maintain odds.

Dialoguing with evil
Painting it rainbow
Chatting with war
Pleading for peace
The peace they are killing.

Large subterfuge of common sabotage
Uncommon camouflage of long subterfuge
Abounding in sabotage.

They dialogue with terrorists
And pamper terror
But they shoot protesters
And kill demonstrators,
Those that are unhappy over their rule.

They shoot those who carry placards
And dialogue with those who bear arms.

VICTIMS

Victims, all around
In mournful mood
Perpetual tears
Eternal traumas
A drama of leadership.

Senseless, careless, lifeless
Motionless, remorseless
Lives, go down the drain.

Living in fears, denying tears
Growing in doubts, fanning war
Victims, victims of hate, victims of tribe
Victims of selfishness, victims of religion
Victims of greed, victims of politics.

Victimization of victims
Selected victims, victims of fate
A fate so satanic
Brought upon them by humans.

First, they make you victim
Then, they fight you
They victimize your struggle
And stigmatize your identity,
Victims from vultures
Volcanic victims of venomous victors.

Ngozi Olivia Osuoha

WIDOWS

Widows abound
Young and old
Those whose husbands were killed
The soldiers who paid the supreme price.

Widows, young and untimely
Those whose husbands were forced to die
Unnecessary deaths; controllable.

Like film tricks, they imagine
They look and wonder
They assume it is not true
But in the end, it is a sad reality.

These widows battle with home
Loneliness, training of children, school fees
They feel lost and abandoned
They doubt the existence of God.

Widows, green blood
Ushered into the hood of boredom.

They face life and its tragedies alone
Lonely nights, terrible advances from all
Saboteurs sabotaging love and patriotism,
A camouflaging piece of human failures.

ORPHANS

Orphans everywhere
Dead parents, gone relatives
Hopeless and helpless children
Moaping at life and death.

Stunted growth
Arrested development
Street life, child labour
More vulnerable, more forgotten.

Orphans of war, orphans of insurgency
Deprived of education and love
Snatched from humanity
Fired, bruised, abused and broken.

Short peace, long night, hot day
Harsh cold, thundering rain, dehumanizing society.

Orphans, victims of terrorism
Victims of stigmatization and terrorization
Innocent, poor, children, meek and mild.

Ngozi Olivia Osuoha

LONELY LOVERS

Lonely lovers at nights
Rolling from pillow to pillow
Warming the bed alone.

Lonely lovers at noon
Trekking, fighting, shooting in the forest
Struggling to be alive the next minute.

Fears and fears at home
Prayers and incense, burning
Sleepless nights, worries and needs
Wishing, waiting, longing, needing, wanting.

Lonely lovers far apart
In worlds apart, partly absurd
Wild, wide and weird
Thoughts running over.

Lonely lovers going crazy
Carrying guns with tears
Shooting in doubts
Families; lost and gone.

BREADWINNERS

These people are breadwinners
Winners of bread for families
Families of loved ones.

They go, beyond reach
Reaching for defense
Reaching for peace
But they return no more awhile.

Breadwinners, being tossed about
Tossed as though they are vagabonds
Treated as if they are not humans.

Hunger, hunger for love
Thirst, thirst for home
Anger, rage for unity
Bitterness, bitterness for rights
Vengeance, vengeance for humiliation.

Ngozi Olivia Osuoha
DROP OUT FROM SCHOOL

Some children drop out
They drop out of school
They hawk, they tout
They fall victims, victims of rape.
Some become trafficked
Some go for slavery
Some run into killers
Some turn addicts
Some via off the society,
Camouflage, a metre rule of subterfuge.

These children lose care
Because a parent or both are gone
They become loose
Loosely influenced and intimidated.

Some grow worse
Some become good, rarely though
But these orphans or dropouts
Seldom actualize their potentials.

Camouflage, subterfuge, sabotage
Grave massage to some ego.

BLOWING UP SELF

For those who blow themselves
Just to save their brothers
The soldiers who give it all
To keep others safe,
We say thank you.

When the enemy advances
And danger is imminent
When capturing is inevitable
Or dying non negotiable,
For the ones who lay down
And decide to blow themselves up
That others might crawl to safety
We salute, we appreciate.

The camouflage, a subterfuge
A tale of head and tail
Felony of fate,
A disaster of life and death
Taunting nations of diverse tongues.

SACRIFICES

Low morale, poor equipments
Poor salary, inferior ammunition
Obsolete arsenal, doubting hope
Yet, you sacrifice for us.

They sacrifice you to ride
They fish you to dive
They trap you to swim
They interweave and intertwine you
For selfish interests, solely
Yet you truck along.

Faithful, hopeful, willful, pride
Loyal, humble, bold and ready
Vigilant, gallant, dedicated, committed
A sacrifice worth appreciating.

Great men of stupendous valour
Rare strength of uncontrollable weight
Dignity and labour of irrevocable price,
Only fools underrate your sacrifices.

TRUE SOLDIERS

For the true soldiers
The ones who toil daily
Those who defend us
Those who guard our land, coasts and air
Your reward is eternal.

Yes, for those ones
Though we know them not
They know themselves
Heaven too, knows them
Not a bit of your sweat, not a drop
Shall go unpaid for.

Dead, alive, unborn
Remembered, celebrated, forgotten
Known, unknown, seen, unseen
The land of our forefathers
And the footsteps of our ancestors
Shall grant you peace.

For the true soldiers
Nothing shall take your peace,
Your souls shall find love in heaven.

Ngozi Olivia Osuoha

BORROW-PIT

Yes, for the stories we hear
And the pictures we see
For the videos and online news
For those innocent people killed
The ones shot into pits,
The young men, wasted secretly
And the bodies discovered,
For the corpses that are untraceable
The camouflage camouflages.

Those shot in bushes and forests
Those told to run for their lives
Only to be shot and killed while obeying
For those thrown into rivers.

For all unthinkable and unbelievable news
Propaganda, rumours, stories and events
Those unjustly camouflaged
Unforgettable, unforgettable, unforgettable.

But blood speaks, blood speaks
Yes, your blood speaks,
We hear, we hear you.

CAPTURED SOLDIERS

Captured soldiers by the enemy
The caricature of the nation
Vented all anger on them.

Tortured beyond human
Raped beyond animal
Torn and worn out
Dismembered and maimed
Slit, stabbed, butchered.

Captured soldiers, wish uncreated
Prisoners of war, scapegoats
Born of men and women
Treated like beasts and monsters,
Cooked and boiled by aliens.

Lovers in the dark
Relatives, at loss
Nations mourn
The camouflage, camouflages on and on.

Ngozi Olivia Osuoha

EJECTION FROM THE BARRACKS

When you die and go
Your families mourn and grieve
Your relatives wander afar
Then the mourning begins.

Ejection from the barracks
Little or nowhere to go
School, business, trade
And many more; tiny.

Gratuity, pension, accrued rights
Compensation, honour or the like
All hanging, pending timelessly.

Widows and fatherless children
Helpless and hopeless for ages
Wonders appearing like drama.

The poor roof under their head
The last hope, the last
No one dares care,
As they leave for no return.

UNKNOWN SOLDIER

This is for all the soldiers
Those who died somewhere hidden
The ones whose grave were unknown
Neither seen, heard, nor officially buried
We remember you all.

The one devoured by beasts
The one starved to death
The one tortured death
The one who lost their way
The one who died in the forest
The one it took ages to return,
The one that should not have died
The one that met his death unawares.

Wherever your graves be
In the forests, bush, valleys, mountains
In strange lands, borders, seas
In deserts, oceans, prisons
Wherever you died and when
However death snatched you,
Whatever be your wish and prayers
This is for you all
We remember you, unforgettable
We appreciate you all.

Rest, sleep still
Peace, be thy rest
Thy bones live and survive
Because thy labour is not vain.

No matter the sabotage and camouflage
No matter the subterfuge,
You are true heroes
Death feared you.

You were never cowards
Those who betrayed you, were.

Ngozi Olivia Osuoha

INTERNALLY DISPLACED PERSONS' CAMPS (IDP CAMPS)

Orphans, widows and widowers
Men, women and children
Young and old
Learned, unlearned, great and small
Displaced, internally and externally.

No privacy, no peace, no joy
Just survival of the fittest
Struggling for a meal
Despite monies mapped out,
The subterfuge; a camouflage.

Women giving birth in unsafe arenas
Babies not assured of surviving
Bombs and guns; terrorizing
War, hunger, famine, thirst.

Internally displaced people everywhere
Camps of dirty premises
Eyesores and ungodly scenes
Fates and destinies interwoven
Fears and hates, intertwined
Nothing actually makes senses.

AID WORKERS

For all the health workers murdered
For all captured and tortured
Men and women of humanitarian services
Paid and unpaid
We pray for your souls.

For the doctor from my hometown
The orphan that made brilliant result
For the unknown star, dimmed
The Catholic faithful
The bright full moon
The one with United Nations
Killed in the North East
Dr Onyekachi Izuogu
You lived three decades plus
And they killed you in March, 2018
This book too is for your memorial,
Rest well dear, may your ancestors show you love
May they be happy and warm on your arrival,
And your God; a dwelling place.

For others, known and unknown
Men and women, from wherever
Killed for humanity
We immortalize your souls here.

Ngozi Olivia Osuoha

TORTURED

For the victims of terror
And those displaced
Those troubled and hunted
The ones tortured
Mentally, physically, economically
Politically, religiously, socially, educationally
Those who lost uncountable things;
May you find rest.

Children, innocent children
Teens, poor teens
Teenagers of blossoming strengths
Finding the world full of hate
Full of anger, rage, and harshness
May you discover peace.

Chopped off fingers
Cut off legs
Crushed bones
Bruised heads
Perforated skin
Flogged, electrocuted
Frog-jumped, raped, punished
Inflicted pains, burnt flesh
Abducted, kidnapped, freed
Captured, killed, forgotten
May you rest in Paradise.

BETRAYED

With trust and faith in your land
You march in strength and zeal
Suppressing your fear
Buttressing your morale
Struggling to live
Fighting to win
Trying to stay afloat
Giving in your best
But, someone, a ghost appears.

The betrayer, the monster
The greedy Python
The crocodile, marine spirit
The selfish chameleon
The green snake on the green grass
The camouflager and saboteur
The betrayer, the ingrate.

He is there, amidst the fight
Fighting the fighters
Tightening the escape routes
And being bent on his interest
Holding on to his grip,
Making sure his pocket is filled
The betrayer, Judas and his kiss.

The end someday is real
And we shall find out,
Because Judas was never sainted.

Ngozi Olivia Osuoha

AMBUSHED

Always ambushed, waylaid
It baffles and shocks
How a faceless foe attacks
How he takes leverage,
How his boldness increases.

Capturing coasts, falling cities
Advancing, retreating, reinforcing
Firing, without ceasing fire
Fearless, mean, sophisticated
Blunt, audacious, outrageous
Non relenting, non reluctant, non assuming
Determined, dedicated, committed
Bent on harming, killing, destroying
It bewilders the ordinary

Must they ambush,
Must they waylay,
Who feeds them news
Who informs them of movement,
Who fights government
And why are governments with loopholes?

BEHEADED

Soldiers run out of bullets
Out of guns and weapons
Soldiers get surrounded
Sometimes, they surrender
Directly, indirectly, individually and or collectively,
Taken as spoils.

Yes, spoils of war
War of terrorism,
They know nothing anymore
Because God may not perform a miracle.

These ones are unlucky
As even an equipped soldier can do nothing at this moment.

Lo, life and death
The latter likely glittering.

Most of them beheaded
As beheading enlivens the foe
Blood, blood upon blood
Happy, happier, they become.

Heads of heroes, heroes, great men
Men who might have been betrayed or sold out.

Ngozi Olivia Osuoha

BOMBED AND BURNT

Bombed unawares
Blown up in pieces,
Burnt in numbers
Shot at strategic places
Killed in trenches
Rounded in locations
Caught up in patrols
Always in a drama,
Leaving the nation in traumatic dilemma.

Pictures, photos, news, stories
Videos, tapes, feelings, assumptions
Imaginations, experiences, reports
Rumours, defences, projections
Postulates, theories, chances, possibilities
Foundations, politics and calculations
One wonders where it happens!

A kingdom divided against itself falls
Two cannot walk nor work together except they agree,
None can serve two masters at once
This fight glitters like gold
It scares the blind
It worries the dumb,
It forces the lame to run
If we continue this way
There may not be a land like ours soon.

THE COINAGE

The coinage is worrisome
The head is aching
It is piercing the eyes
And biting the ears,
It torments the mouth
And bleeds the nose,
The teeth in deep anguish
The hands, shiver
The legs hurt
The stomach burns
The heart breaks
The soul is down
The spirit wanders
The mind is overwhelmed
The bone is weak
The flesh is melted,
The system is sick
The body is dying
Wake up, heal this man
For the grave is welcoming him.

Rise up, rise up, the bloodshed
The land rages
The gods weep
The sky mourns
The clouds darken
And the darkness is thick,
Thicker than blood.

Ngozi Olivia Osuoha

The coinage is sabotage
The sabotage is camouflage,
The camouflage is subterfuge
The subterfuge is such a coinage.

The subterfuge, horrible
Horrible land of unknown end
End, that is seen yet unseen.

The subterfuge is a click
A clique of carnivorous cabal
Cabalistic canal
Canonizing and moisturizing haze,
Haze of immaculate immunity,
A subterfuge; unimaginable.

Build this land, heal her
Rebuild these walls for the living
For the unborn is vowing not to come
Because the dead has told a horrible story
Story, that is truly beyond hell,
Beyond the world of the unborn.

The Subterfuge

Ngozi Olivia Osuoha

about the author

Ngozi Olivia Osuoha is a Nigerian poet, writer and thinker. A graduate of Estate Management with experience in Banking and Broadcasting.

She has published eleven poetry books and co-authored one (with Kenyan literary critic Amos O. Ojwang').

She has featured in more than forty international anthologies and also has published over two hundred and fifty poems and articles in over twenty countries.

Many of her poems have been translated and published into other languages, including Spanish, Romanian, Khloe, Farsi, and Arabic, among others.

She has won many awards; she is a one time *Best of the Net* nominee, and she has numerous words on marble.

www.ingramcontent.com/pod-product-compliance
Lightning Source LLC
Chambersburg PA
CBHW030122100526
4491CB0000B/497